more praise for
HOT THICKET

"What does it mean to be both orphan and animal? Cassandra Rockwood Ghanem's *Hot Thicket* lives at the heart of this question. This book rejects fathers, paternal violence, the havoc wreaked by the state and history, emerging from the ash of countless deaths as a bright moving flame. An inventory of loss, this tenderly imagistic collection renders its grief objects softly even as their teeth are unbearably sharp. I find myself at this book's end, dreaming of its torn violets and jarred butterflies, and also longing to be liberated."

Muriel Leung
author of *Imagine Us, The Swarm*

"Cassandra Rockwood Ghanem's poetry reveals big truths—her truth—with words that simultaneously capture the past and present to convey her story. The imagery is vivid, full of knowledge, and with a deep realization of life experiences, some processed and some still raw. The way Cassandra weaves words is more than a simple art, it is like seeing aspects of her life through a lens as she lives. Don't be surprised if this book of poetry sticks with you long after you first read it. "

Jerry Cimino
founder of The Beat Museum

NOMADIC PRESS

OAKLAND

111 FAIRMONT AVENUE
OAKLAND, CA 94611

BROOKLYN

475 KENT AVENUE #302
BROOKLYN, NY 11249

WWW.NOMADICPRESS.ORG

MASTHEAD

FOUNDING PUBLISHER
J. K. FOWLER

ASSOCIATE EDITOR
MICHAELA MULLIN

EDITOR
MAW SHEIN WIN

DESIGN
JEVOHN TYLER NEWSOME

MISSION STATEMENT

Through publications, events, and active community participation, Nomadic Press collectively weaves together platforms for intentionally marginalized voices to take their rightful place within the world of the written and spoken word. Through our limited means, we are simply attempting to help right the centuries' old violence and silencing that should never have occurred in the first place and build alliances and community partnerships with others who share a collective vision for a future far better than today.

INVITATIONS

Nomadic Press wholeheartedly accepts invitations to read your work during our open reading period every year. To learn more or to extend an invitation, please visit: www.nomadicpress.org/invitations

DISTRIBUTION

Orders by teachers, libraries, trade bookstores, or wholesalers:

Nomadic Press Distribution
orders@nomadicpress.org
(510) 500-5162
nomadicpress.org/store

Small Press Distribution
spd@spdbooks.org
(510) 524-1668 / (800) 869-7553

This book was made possible by a loving community of chosen family and friends, old and new.

For author questions or to book a reading at your bookstore, university/school, or alternative establishment, please send an email to info@nomadicpress.org.

Cover art: Arthur Johnstone

Published by Nomadic Press, 111 Fairmount Avenue, Oakland, California 94611

First printing, 2022

Library of Congress Cataloging-in-Publication Data

Title: *Hot Thicket*
p. cm.
Summary: *Hot Thicket*, is a poetic journey through interpersonal and societal wildfires. With the turn of each page, the heat slowly rises as small children cry out against the patriarchy, modern-day colonizers are held in check, and the planet itself is given a platform to voice millennia of abuse and desecration. Within the burning passages, Cassandra Rockwood Ghanem illuminates hidden truths with flames of a different kind, flames lit to incinerate an outmoded culture of ignorance and denial.

[1. POETRY / Subjects & Themes / Healing. 2. POETRY / Middle Eastern. 3. POETRY / Women Authors. 4. POETRY / American / General.] I. III. Title.

LIBRARY OF CONGRESS CONTROL NUMBER: 2021949445

ISBN: 978-1-955239-18-9

HOT THICKET

CASSANDRA ROCKWOOD GHANEM

HOT THICKET

CASSANDRA ROCKWOOD GHANEM

CONTENTS

introduction

Table of Contents	1
Chills	4
Madrone Mouth	5
Elephant Burial	7
Shadow Box	10
Thickness	12
The Last Time I Walked w/ the Flame Thrower	14
Mount Lebanon	16
New Growth	18
Covert	19
Lost Neighbors	24
The Sun Gashes	26
About to Bleed	27
Speak of Violets	29
The Flock	32
Rock Crab Empty Moon	34
The Felled I	37
The Felled II	38

The Felled III 40
The Felled IV 42
The Felled V 44
The Physics of Desertion 47
What to Look For 54
Broken Lacrymatory 55

reading guide

INTRODUCTION

"What is to give light must endure burning"
Victor Frankl

When I was a teenager, this quote brought me a lot of solace, mostly because I knew the path set out before me was not going to be easy or well-traversed. When I reflect on this quote now, I recognize the potential hazard of it. There is inherent risk in inhabiting this perspective when there is a tendency, particularly in schools of "Western" thought, to idealize tropes such as bootstrapping and martyrdom—where one must endure immense suffering, or burning if you will, in order to reach some, often unattainable future goal, or pave the way for others' liberation. This mindset has enabled a lot of unnecessary struggle, violence, and destruction in my own life and in the lives of countless others.

Meanwhile, there are philosophers, writers, lovers, artists and dreamers, who, in the pursuit of a deepend state of consciousness, invite a different kind of fire, invite the destruction of their ego, invite the dissolution of a false, inflated sense of self, in an attempt to further understand all of humankind. In this form, enduring the fire(pain) one feels when they realize and accept their own mistakes and missteps often leads to a greater capacity for giving light—through a purified, more compassionate and empathetic existence. Fire, in this metaphorical sense,

can have so many meanings and representations.

I invite you, as you read through the poems in *Hot Thicket*, to think about how the fire moves through it, and in turn, how it moves through you. What can we do, collectively, to create more of the flames that burn away illusions, and less of those that destroy innocence and beauty?

TABLE OF CONTENTS

When your life is marked by traumatic events
And each memory holds within it
A location
A violation
A part of the body
What someone told you when you said something
How they framed and reframed
Asked for more
Or didn't
Wanted you to stop making yourself look like a victim
Wanted you to stop being so bold
Wanted you to focus more on resilience
Wanted a happier ending
Preferred the metaphor
Preferred the silence
Told you not to call it by its name
Told you to give it another name
And when you did, when you called it teeth, that wasn't the right one
And when you called it flora, that had already been done
How do you make chapters
Add titles
Separate one thing from the next in an ouroboros of returning
When a new pain is inflicted by the same mouth

When the same pain is inflicted by a different mouth
When you're reminded of what occured
How does that not become something fresh
How is a vicarious trauma not your own trauma
How does the child not witness the mother and become her
The child is writing on the wall what the mother is writing on the child's back
Who gets to tell the child what it knows about cycles of violence
When page five is also the same as page fifty five, just years apart, or generations apart
When the father's hands find their way into everything
When the father wants to use your own hands to write him a new name
When the priest wants that, too
When there's a correlation between the abuse of earth and the abuse of women and children
And you try to make music out of it, but the record keeps skipping
And you're walking a different path but the same flowers grow there
When the way it became a movie in your head wasn't acceptable
When they called you a trauma pornographer
Because it doesn't suit their gaze
Then they ask you to submit
To include a table of contents or turn it into a memoir
Make it represent the whole of you, at least, so they can call you damaged

Give each page its own title, so they can categorize it
And it begins to remind you of slut-shaming or victim-blaming
Wear a longer skirt, they say, and bad things won't happen
Show less skin, be more ladylike
But you know that's how this started in the first place
How it began before you were born
The order of things has always been your undoing
So instead you give them more of what they don't approve of
You give them your version of the story
How one afternoon in a park is only survivable if you turn it into a one-act play
How the spirit knows how to fly above the body, yes, but that's when the child is no more
And you do it even though you won't get the same accolades that a man does for telling his version
And you do it even though they'll try to invade and invalidate it
And you do it even though it'll be rejected so many times for so many different reasons
Because these are your contents
And you didn't put them there
It's time to expose them to the light of day
Return them to their senders
It's time to put them on the table

CHILLS

Those first times, when you were behind me,
I felt something cool always
watching from the brush.

Think heavy cream.
Think California rivers in goldrush days.
Think of where music fans meet the stage.
Think of the way your pleasure might look
when it hasn't been expressed for weeks.

At one point you wanted finches
to rise from the shrubs when you touched me.

As if seasons could be changed by migrations.
But it's the other way around.

MADRONE MOUTH

How can I mind my own business
when the child is speaking

and the thing coming out of her mouth
is more twisted than an old Madrone,

orange and crimson,
and that sinuous thin bark

is flaking off of her lips
as they try to tell her,
"This shit just happens."

You wouldn't send her out at midnight
with those spindly foalish legs of hers

to fetch yesterday's mail
from the box at the end of the drive

even if you were dirt poor
and waiting on a fat check,

but you leave her in the care
of questionable hands

and then try to burn it down
when the whole wrangled

and complicated thicket
appears on her tongue.

ELEPHANT BURIAL

I revisit the mark where you once lied,
slow moving eyes creasing like an aerial riverbed.

Dream walks along that mother river,
in and out of hotels with peeling walls.

I end up in other countries
listening to wise boys run on dirt roads.

My friends are all there in small boats,
they are seeing the sky but they don't see me.

Lighting fires for reflections in water,
humming into hands,

I don't know if it's shock or cold
they are trying to avoid.

Priests once led us in processions
where we drank fermented flowers,

washed bodies of lost ones.
I would have washed you

even of the pain I painted with
had you given me the chance.

We forgot to tie our fingers tightly with red string
and cut it with an axe.

We forgot to mix the ashes with food,
or wrap them in fresh muslin,

so we could dance around the tomb to live music.
I covered my eyes and felt my hands becoming marigolds.

It will never be time to turn my bones
with the bones of others you left behind.

Hold me skyward and shout,
I give you back to your life!

We should have held these things first,
like elephants do, unflinching fascination,

mulling over dead selves, recognizing
what it was we killed in one another.

I'll keep a lace of your hair around my neck for a year.
Say my name — then don't say it anymore.

Smear cliffs you visit, river stones, and the inside
of natural caves bright cinnabar red.

Serve intoxicating drinks when you say
that you once loved me — otherwise don't say it at all.

Unlike elephants, most animals don't hesitate
to leave the weak behind.

But elephant herds, we take good care,
we search among fronds for dropped flowers

and never let our loved ones suffer
a thoughtless goodbye.

SHADOW BOX

Shelburne Falls is a little town in Western Mass. partially hydro-powered by a damned waterfall, where I spent preschool years hiding behind floral skirts and dodging grease-laden men in suspenders and muscle shirts; one day we gathered nets to capture Monarchs hatching from green chrysalides and walked the Bridge of Flowers, passing over the town dam; their new wings sparkled, iridescent in places and powdery in others; I held the jar; my mother rolled a joint and smoked in the rocking chair as haze filled the room, setting sunbeams pressed through the blinds like dusty two-by-fours; their wings slowed and faded down to autumn leaves; my mother pulled out a bag of cotton balls and a bottle of liquid and she put the jar on the coffee table; the butterflies woke and fluttered; after pouring some of the liquid on cotton balls, she opened the jar lid just enough to drop them inside, and as they slipped down the glass, wings heaving and glinting, everything eventually closed up together like hands in prayer; I don't know how much I asked, or even if I knew how to ask about what was going on, but I remember my heart pounding in my chest the same way it would in later years when I'd come home to find her slumped on the couch, lost in altered states, jars and bottles hidden at her side, and how I knelt on the rug wide-eyed, gripping the wooden table, long after she was finished; I sat staring at the duller underside of everything, wondering if the vibrance was forever buried; and before bed, she would wrench the velvety wings open, glue them in places where violence showed, and pin them on satin covered foam, to later slide it all into a glass box; a stoic radiance loomed hovered over the sofa, an emblem of the first time I'd witness death. The ache I learned to write by.

THICKNESS

I remember the first time I felt
Thick legs envelop me
A big belly on my belly
Buddha-like
Puffed-out-bird-chest-like
Pushy and fresh with
Silky soft arms encircling me
You know it's a sort of majesty
How a little fatness owns
Whatever it hovers over
How a little fat
Defies everything
And how I've always adored rebels
Lovely little edge dwellers
Spilling over the boundary lines
Coloring outside the boxes
Bold body wisdom doing what it will
And the hot water can't take it under
A round man like a mother goddess
A man like a faience figurine
A woman moving everyone with her size
We siphon everything in
Regal, spongey creatures

Hold my roundness in your roundness
We will step into the great expanses
And take our space

THE LAST TIME I WALKED WITH THE FLAME THROWER

When summer ends I reflect on the last time I walked with the flame
 thrower.
I knew to stay away by then, my skin scorched and keloid
in places where embers had lodged.

He said he was out of lighter fluid, this time.
He said, *Sorry*, (he knew how hard the infernos had been on me).
It was a long winter. I told him how I barely moved until spring,

even then my lungs were smoke-filled for months at the thought of leaving.
But how I easily forget the way he vanished in the monsoon, how he
would not come if there was even a chance of rain. Of course

when they told me to invite my angels in, that's when I called,
that was when hunting season began, that was when I learned
about the two kinds of light determined by a distance in between.

He told me there'd be berries in the deep arid woods. Parched,
my mouth watered and I felt like a desperate creature.
The entire woods will be full of berries, he said, Let's go!

His lips were bright crimson stained and incandescent within.
We went into the tinder, kindling cracking beneath our feet.
It won't be long now, he motioned, *Come,*

blueberries will burst between your teeth, black raspberries
so tart and plump they drip when you touch them.
See, he said, and as he turned toward me, I could see his tongue,

a match lit to consume everything.

MOUNT LEBANON

Bees surround her face, drink nectar
from beads of sweat on her crown,

we rest our heads, one by one,
on her chest without observation.

Amulet of citrus in April, thistle
and honeydew in June, her scrawl

is found on cedar trees, leaves of juniper,
crystalline etchings in natural sugar.

Violent winds rouse red earth as she hurls
herself in the vermillion river.

And we have grape leaves
to wrap the rice in,
tobacco for the waterpipe,
wheat fields spanning feral as her hair.

Voiceless Jezebel looks on with olivine eyes,
to the once blue seas where men had sailed
and returned to scorn her gifts as lies,
feed her to dogs and demon kings,

because when a woman held power,
her command was, *Above all, worship nature.*
And they decided this was the worst possible sin.

She appears tonight as cars go still on every curb,
shrouded in a blanket of pollen and seed pods.

The churches are empty now, darlings,
towering buildings go vacant and dim.

Across the years without the sour haze
that hides the stars, we can hear her

on these evenings, so free the moon
once again hears night birds'

songs and lone sounds rising,
like the deserted oud player,
and the lost daughter of Mount Lebanon,
she strums and sings,
We'll not forget,

Shukran, Shukran, Shukran

اركش اركش اركش

NEW GROWTH

For Alexandra Najjar (January 26, 2017–August 4, 2020)

She brought them to a corridor of time-weathered limestone
walls singing with water that feeds a distant rush
and she pointed to a garden below of entirely black trees

and as their eyes adjusted they saw black olives and purple-black figs
black grape leaves and sour sage drenched in black blood-like
pomegranate syrups and honey the color of squid ink

thyme sumac cumin dark as licorice and rich with smoky aromas
black rice pools of black tea bundles of black garlic and black beans

black pepper covering black lentils on a bed of black trumpet mushrooms
black sesame seeds piled high on ashy wild farrow burnt vermillion
kale coaly citrus and apricots fresh as midnight sky

a garden planted on the ram's watch a garden planted after the famines
damp and sticky as pitch and the child's voice came in desperate
questions:
Why do people kill each other? When is it our time to live?

COVERT

Who were you
before ships became your shoes?

Now you sway on mesozoic legs
wondering why there's no stability inside.

I heard you pierced ears with knives and severed
free thinking on every continent before.

Here you find dissolution sung by virgins and bird-god
voices, often dressed like men to make you listen.

When you arrived, you raised a flag
ensigned with the last heart you ate

just to let us know you were in the harbor.
Now you make a crown that resembles it

and tell everyone to stay put for a body count.
You say, *Drink and be merry!* offering barrel-aged tears

from a lost pleasure shore, calling casualties saviors,
only so long as their names serve as snares.

When the last remaining bridges have been burned
and the rivers run dry, then you'll beg:

But wait, see how beautiful your heart would look on a stick?
You could be the next flag stake on my territory of ladders!

HOT AIR

It's one of those moments I want to grasp at,
the feeling: a ship tilting too far on waves,
nothing to grab on to, lurching.

Motioning with hither-hands
he cuts my thoughts to splinters.
Do you have a girlfriend? I ask.

He's married, but won't admit it.
I'm free, he says,
so we drive up to the peak under stars,

Let me show you how to pour water,
devoted, as women do, he purrs.
We use a dirty coffee mug. I lift it to the sky

and watch the moon shine through a murky stream.
In the morning we walk by Caffe Trieste as passersbys
snap us with cameras. He leans into me,

They always take pictures of me here, he says.
At the bar, he rolls his pant leg to expose a bruise—
damage from the clumsiness of his rage.

When he says, *Kiss me*, how I watch him there,
my insides operating like a broken math game—
an equation with a populace of answers
clanking against throat and gut—
but only one solution.

One more try, I think, try to understand.
A million flaneurs in and he selects me?
Why do you love me so much, he asks me

after he asks his wife the same question.
And she, with boughs of sorrow, cloaked with purpose,
waits for him to finish finishing another woman

so that he can redeem himself in her arms.
And after all of these years, women become gifts
for her—a consolation. I am the prize.
Top-notch. Heck, I am the ten-year anniversary diamond!
He will destroy me and she knows it.
He grins, serrated mouth a cat's
in the shade under his hat,

he brushes his cheek against mine,
and whispers hotly, *I would have married you*

if I met you first.

LOST NEIGHBORS

The way they have to hover
over insurmountable streets,

pavement their river, living rooms
of briny cafes, a basement

on Telegraph, beetlejuice vista
on Stanford, an underground

passageway (rabbit hole
only mused about).

The bathroom is anywhere
two doors can be opened,

a shower is hands clasped
around hands under the freeway.

Those naked wear mist
lit orange by too much city.

Once admired for their grace
and humility, they blinked

and became circadian fighters.
New people with new money

took their places, forced them to make homes
of odd things, trash finds: boards, carts,

barber pole rings, red tights, trash bags
their round eyes rely on openness at night.

They are the last who fling themselves
upon the obtuse of our proliferating

ignorance, arms and legs flung wide,
wider holding our greedy

concrete in their teeth,
considered weeds by the elite.

THE SUN GASHES

our nostalgia, ugly joy
Sunday crisp-cotton
pressed, ready for
gospel in a temple
missing gods

our children ache like tomatoes
soft, unacquainted with their
messiness. Here, in a village
overrun with paradise

our bare children run
rocky paths, in shining eyes
a specific hunger

only here it is not so much a
shortage of food as it is a
shortage of fathers.

ABOUT TO BLEED

On the hutch part of her water
    bed frame were little round pot seeds.

I touched them, put them
    in my mouth like popcorn
kernels, stared off at the unemployed
    typewriter on the screen porch, and lay there
on my back, the plastic undulating
    beneath me, considering what
to make my little brother for dinner.

Some days her room was different, blinds
    rolled up and devoid of the strange sour after
smell of uncommon smoke.

Off the cuff, I found my almost 90's pink Levi's
    Christmas divulged premature
on a latch-key afternoon. MTV's Madonna
    in leather was raping a chair
in a slit of door cracked on the living room.
    I tried them on. I danced like her.
It was 1989.

Eventually, through the cupboards
    I established her huge
jug of Carlo Rossi, I licked it from my pinky
    pink and tart. Everything was suddenly
copper and wet, rosy like that wine
    and sharp, about to bleed.

On the tail-end of ten that November, I stuck
    my chilly fingers in the holes
of everything, the old brass Massachusetts
    locks, into the folds
of her braided rug, the one Great
    Grandmother made when I was born.
It was ripping.

SPEAK OF VIOLETS

She spoke of violets she was given
as a child, her voice tight, unhappy.

He violated me, she said
with violets in her throat.

Years later she gave me the books—
what men did in the book made me

think of the giver of her violets
I get the story, I thought.

When I was seventeen, I tasted
a violet for the first time

drank too much wine at a party
he followed me upstairs

I woke in a t-shirt, head-aching dizzy
salty violets in my mouth

wet lavender between my thighs.
Friends were watching a movie downstairs,

they said the floorboards creaked
all night. I saw the sheets I woke in dyed

deep amethyst—sweet violets fell
from the ceiling, that was the morning fun

began to sound like bedpost, like wood.
Six years later, my boss force-fed me

blossoms in exchange for a job
he kissed me with velvety flowers

as I cried, told me to drink dirty bouquets,
for weeks I was drenched in fear

every shade of blue and purple.
Now I know how they taste, bitter

like baking soda, smell of sweat and dirt,
sound of wood and metal—soft petals

feel like a pressure that won't let up.
I feel it when someone walks behind

me to my car, violet sororia roots
violating me long after footsteps

disappear—I pluck them stem stamen,
from my tender areolas, labia, lips,

scratch tear at an embedded garden
sprung, heart-shaped, asymmetrical

blooming from violent times, johnny
jump-up, pansy frightened even

of the dappled shade, listening
to sounds outside my window

at night, spitting violets
tasting for metal, always

concerned someone might arrive

to visit me

with more flowers.

THE FLOCK

Watching the entrance of an old mine shaft by Sulphur Creek where bats swirl in atomic circles, I never wished death on you, only healing, and you drank so much, spewing coils of words percolated by a red hot whisky demon who slashed my tires night after night when I finally said goodbye, and my body held it, hollow with worry, teeming with endangered bats that spin and cross over one another as darkness descends, each one, a memory of something said, each one, a concern about what's to come, like that night we watched films in your parents' basement, the devil came and called me a wayfaring whore, threw me across the room because I wouldn't fuck you, like the night he told me you had blood on your hands, but would never say why, of course the sun rose, too, in your world, and those who met the mask basked in a blinding light, but tonight I wait impatiently as it slowly shirks behind parched hills, a mountain lion stalks a weak, dehydrated California quail who stays late upon the canyon wall in one moment, and in the next, my chest opens wide as the night sky, while one by one the bats, who long overstayed their welcome, whirring and circling with ever increasing urgency, escape in all directions, carrying thoughts that only lingered because you remained, and that predator walked the ridge, companion only to the sharp, stubborn sunbeams of a dry summer, your silhouette seen downing liquor and pills, unknowingly watching for whatever was weary, and thirsty, like you, and alone, and I don't know how you died, and I don't rejoice, but as the flock leaves the mine, headed out toward the stars, dipping and diving after leafhoppers and caddisflies, I hear something new, a fiery piano being played across the steppe, a sudden song so familiar but never before, so I walk that way to where a young woman is singing, her voice is brave and innocent and alight, and in this moment my chest becomes a furnace, first, and then so vacant and open that it vibrates with her one long endnote, and it doesn't stop.

ROCK CRAB EMPTY MOON

Seasons embellish our arciform bodies,
outstretched on Bolinas Beach

we reinvent cellular memories in waves,
how many stories did we run from

on the cutting-edge of rebirth,
only to find their origins

nested in the palms of our hands?
We passed up the pleasure there, too.

A crab claw on the sand
reminds me that I already let go;

we are sitting where I sat with other lovers,
they snaked around my body

like only the wind does now,
they burned me

like the sun is burning me now,
and the voice inside me spoke

same as their criticisms.
We read books and crunch honey crisp apples.

It's a new moon, I say, *but why do we call it new?*
It's a clean slate, you say,

even the light needs to be swept away sometimes,
and then you leave again.

THE FELLED I

"Most human predators, however, seek power, not food.
To destroy or damage something is to take its power."
Gavin de Becker, The Gift of Fear

Plants sense danger. They can hear
the difference between wind and hunter.

A man, sitting beside me, looks down at the book
he reads and sighs, looks up at the sky, I sympathize:

A fellow-feeling emerges, but the stairs creak
and up comes another man, unsuspecting.

The wind chimes stop ringing.
Tiny mustard plants react to the sound of teeth.

As if they caterpillar up the stairs,
defense chemicals rise, and the foliage becomes

a turn off to the predator.

THE FELLED II

He tells me he pulled the molar
on the right side when it was rotten

proud—he shows me a gap
where smooth flesh arches vacant.

It's a tunnel to something real. I want
to know how it feels—so when our lips meet,

I push my tongue under.
Tiny frond-like energetic arms

sweep around for form and shape.
Together we beg for a controversy

that will make us human again. As his mouth
falls open, for a moment, I think I hear

wind in the valves of his heart.
Instead he is eating all the leaves.

When I was a child, my mother told me to lick
the end of the battery to see if it had a charge—

I tried to stick my tongue in a light socket later
when she wasn't looking, but something different happened:

a tiny, hollow rectangle gave me the sense
that there is a universe behind the walls.

There are scarred places in us both where things catch
and shine in the dark.

Breathing with him I feel his hands search
for a similar place on my body—

something that holds light
a chloroplast, some chlorophyll, to fill himself

with the small bioluminescence remaining in me.
Later I walk the city alone, cold soaked to the bone.

THE FELLED III

Immense networks envelop our forms:
Banyan, Eucalyptus, Oak, Redwood, Sequoia—

if we lean into them, an internet of fungus
communicates with other bodies, electric—

all receptors piqued. A sensory ecosystem
deepens within me, like when water comes

together with other water, once rain, once
stream—now ocean—

this mass of thin threads, Mycelium—
anonymous lives knitted, organically

ignored roots linking one-to-the-next.
The remains of a Banyan tree have valves

and ventricles carrying sounds like wind
chimes—they bleed forever in invisible

incense. It's holy, really.
Braced for water folding over shorelines

in storms or when earthquakes hit,
each loss is a radius of dedicated rain—

a choir of colorful flies descending.
And it's challenging to know the connection—

with no external visible labyrinth of lives
no chants in parallel eyes, no meditation

of the body to follow. And it's challenging
when humanity is disconnected—

a beating heart on the rocks
bloody-early on a Sunday morning
heart like a cock-cry
heart like a large dead tree
heart successively collapsing
like a power outage.

THE FELLED IV

We cut wooden teeth for an unsightly
cringe along the skin. Plants emit

volatile chemical cues, carried in blood
streams to other parts. Easily confused

for excitement, hormones control growth
factors, trigger and regulate how far we go.

And the gardener trims at the top.
(for flowers or for fruit) *But what's the value*

in that? They ask, not wanting to see. The sense
in which we are like trees, like inkblots, filthy

sepia—nostalgic feeling in the dirt
for sweeter times. Endangered while

reproducing compounds mate in
certain ways, natural protective actions

confront predators in pomegranates?
Free radicals in apples? We don't know

what's safe or harmful anymore.
When you meet me with your back up,

the surface of this city is no longer a network.
We become organically blind teethy buildings

amid buildings programmed to be made of teeth.
Gapped, broken, bridged—everything's braced.

THE FELLED V

If comedy were innate in me, I could play the part
they want me to enact. A man walks to the Condor

Topless Bar. Smoke moves from him like a locomotive.
He has no umbrella. He is me. I am him.

Without a mother, without a partner, without lovers—
we are all uncovered, fast, and trying to stay lit.

Concentric circles radiate a network of codes
refractions, heartbeats, and years, like the trees.

But there are four hundred trees per person
and a Eucalyptus alone is older than any of us.

Regardless, we don't learn from sympathetic
structures. We tear things apart, no consolations.

And unlike sea turtles and elephants, our erasures
offer no take-away for the predator here,

there is no shell, no tusk. When some things disappear
all that happens is a radius of quiet expanding,

water meeting other water—this is how it is
without families, without identities, how it feels

for the spirit to be left behind. Everything becomes dangerous.
Every sound is a predator—because a predator is anything

that leaves, and leaving is the only thing with teeth.

THE PHYSICS OF DESERTION

I.

I hear the fatherland rises
again and again like a phoenix,
burnt and rebuilt at least seven times.
Haven't I overcome so much without you?
Is it enough to prove my strain?

I see the orphan image and wonder
if I'll ever get there, Lebanon.
Orphan: phonetically like oar and fan,
one moves through water,
the other through air.

Phoenix-land:
Where prophets once sat beneath cedars
drinking clay-fermented wine,
where mosques and churches
share same streets.

But here, I'm only one of your children deprived.
Equivalent to two young animals that have lost
their father, now running in different directions.
Or three frantic birds, refused some protection from the storm.

I am a first line (as of a paragraph)
separated from text and appearing
at the bottom of a column.
Because what are [we] called if [they] leave?
Is my name thrown violently in sand?
Inhabited like a hermit crab shell?
Only worn as a house robe is (when naked)?

—I have been named
—I have his name
—He gave it to me when I was born
:now see how everyone knows
I belong to him: I belong to Lebanon—
life-breath roused, oar moving through thick air
of unnamed, now mobilized.

▯▯∘
Ancient Phoenicians knew the power of language.
Ancient priestess knew
your princess
[this] princess of Silence

when she speaks heaven shakes
open-mouthed she roars[1]

A great bird folded his wings.
On one knee, he waits
exit sign flashing
cucumber iris full of mint
mouth of pomegranate
language of seeds hard to excavate.
No water for the departed ones
I put the oar in air and nothing happens.

▯▯▯。
The child is born, her parents wrap her in palms, name her:
She is mine. My daughter. My child. My baby.
She has his name. Name. Name. Name. Surname.
See how each word is a bright red petal?

Her botany is identifiable.
In Arab cultures the nisbah is the name
of the ancestral tribe
following a family through generations

but when we are deprived our [name(s)],
when we are severed our [parent(s)],
when we are abandoned:
There is no related text.

I am a familial subgenre,
I am a side street or alley,

I don't even make it on the map.

IV.

Whose eyes are slanting back at me?
I search the black window of the goat eye
I long to walk the temple of Bacchus
I've looked for him in merwah wine

This is the physics of desertion.

Orphan means:
Can I tie my cut rope to you?
Can I fit my puzzle piece to yours?
Might I wet and crosshatch the clay?

Might I fit the slip for bonding?

I scrape off scar and scab
to make a place for place and namesake to enter
Re-opening and always being wet enough
to take a stranger

because who else is there?

V.

Orphan means severance from father—
due to him, severed culture
due to his severed culture.

As one thing cleaves from another, one loss loses another.
A chip off the old block, one third of a world away:
Distance around the world: 24,901 miles.
Distance from San Francisco to Beirut: 7,281 miles.
Distance from my father's heart to mine:
Aleph-naught with no bijective function.

There is no one-to-one, and no number for this,

no relatedness to find the center of one billion times,
no eternity to prove.

The orphan hides behind the pupil.
The orphan is the opposite of infinity.
The orphan is a black hole, pulling so much
that even light is pulled.

With an oar moving into the wind, as from the force
of a fan propelled, I am the only true form of human flotation,
undefinable by laws of physics, this distance I feel
standing next to a woman holding her Lebanese name,
held in fingers lightly since birth like a fig, sweetened
with the honey-musk of her shepherd father,

is the same distance I feel when I map the fathom length
from fingertip-to-fingertip across continent to sea to
continent to sea
so from your skin of bricks
  on the rim of the holy hill   *green as mountains*
you determine fates

whirlpool spins in your river
blowing whirlwinds spawn from your glance

what comes in cannot be equaled
what goes out never ceases[2]

Father,
I'm treading water.
Come take this oar and place a palm in my hand.
Or even just a pit.

Something to keep my mind off the no land in sight.

[1 & 2] Quote translated from the works of Enheduanna, the first known poet.

WHAT TO LOOK FOR

After winter, we would walk on the spongy fields
of our childhood in snow boots, water coming up murky

around blue soles. You'd pull a jackknife from your
shirt pocket and shave the bark, shallow then deep,

revealing a chartreuse layer against strident grays.
The tart pepper of life scent would rise to my nose.

You'd say, *We're at that stage where we can handle*
a damp green wound, remember, leaves will furl open

in spring (and I should know this by now). As you spoke,
I'd take a willowy branch, wring it in opposing circles

until the shiny skin peeled up, pulp fracturing outward
like a paper lantern, sap coruskating brightly within.

This is how we would have prepared to always be holding
on a bit longer, awaiting the life that's yet to be had.

BROKEN LACRYMATORY

I keep wanting to write you a letter,
but instead, I write poems about olives

and figs and cedar. I droll on and on about mountains
and waterfalls, archways and the moon, finding new

contexts, settings, and people to contain them.
And I've come to believe that we could break an amphora

by crying into it together, that we could shatter a tear jar
with our sobs. Imagine a father and daughter who have never met,

for once, standing face-to-face and belonging to each other.
How the world hiccups at that moment, holds its breath,

becomes a lacrymatory for the soul. And it makes me wonder,
Is this my inheritance? A lineage of generations alternately reaching

into the past and then away from it, an arabesque of estrangement.
What if my only request is to hold you before you die?

Why is it easier to board a ship and cross three seas
when I don't believe that we are a people of walls.

Perhaps this silence you gave me is an heirloom, a teacup —
tea leaves, coffee grounds, wine sediments, whichever way

when I gaze steadily and deeply enough into that silence
I find an entire country shaped like my longing.

READING GUIDE

Title: **The Elements**

Throughout history humans have revered the elements with a humbling sense of awe and surrender. Fire, for example, can warm us, and it can create a beautiful painting on the dusky sky — as with a sunset — but it doesn't hesitate to rip through a forest and level it, entirely blind to the creatures finding refuge there.

Which elements have most frequently appeared in your life? This can be metaphorically, symbolically, or in your home environment. How do they inform your spirit?

Prompt

The Elements, in a broad sense, can be Nature, Wind, Air, Water, Fire, Earth, Light, and Darkness/Night (feel free to add your own).

Think comic book-style supernatural powers, think fairytales and myths and gods and goddesses, protagonists and villains, and then let a character in the poem adopt or represent that element.

Representative Poems:

- “The Last Time I Walked With the Flame Thrower” (p.14)
- “The Sun Gashes” (p.26)

Title: **Ancestral Reclamation**

We all come from a lineage of strong, resilient ancestors. Many of our family members endured plagues, famines, colonization, diaspora, slavery, internment, and more.

Some of us have first-hand knowledge of their trials and challenges, but some of us have only glimpses of a much larger story, a story that we cannot ever entirely recover because the hardships that our ancestors endured left no room for record keeping.

Prompt

Write a poem that reflects the rediscovery of your ancestors and/ or ancestral lands.

What does it mean to recover from the tribulations your ancestors endured?

How do you honor and reclaim lost culture?

Think about food, music, dress, healing, spiritual practices, geography, buildings/architectural style, social customs, language, religion and traditions.

Weave your feelings and experiences throughout, and if you'd like to, bring in observations from within your immediate family.

If you want to push yourself even further, turn this poem into a letter or a song.

Representative Poems:

- "Mount Lebanon" (p. 16)
- "The Physics of Desertion" (p. 47)
- "Broken Lacrymatory" (p. 55)

Title: **Writing Trauma**

No one can tell you how, or when, or where to write about traumatic things, but if you feel the urge bubbling up inside you, if it becomes too much to bear, or if you feel catharsis when reading about someone else's experiences and you become inspired, then you know.

To quote the great Maya Angelou, "There is no greater agony than bearing an untold story inside you."

Poetry can be a relief to the internal pressure of holding onto something that was never meant to be yours in the first place.

Prompt

I had an amazing professor and mentor in college, Regina Louise, and when I confessed to her that I had these terrible stories harbored within me, and I didn't know how to write about them because I was so afraid of what people would think, she told me to write them anyway. She said, "Write it all out, every single thing, and don't worry about anyone's opinion. You can revise it later if you need to."

Regina knows! And I am eternally grateful for her wise words.

Use different poetic forms if you like, a list poem, metaphor, hyperbole, etc., but only if it makes it easier for you to write it.

The most important thing is that you respond to your internal guidance and listen to your intuition. Stop when you need to, breathe when you need to, seek out support. Remember, writing about trauma is just one small part of a much larger healing journey.

Representative Poems:

- "Table of Contents" (p. 1)
- "Madrone Mouth" (p. 5)
- "Speak of Violets" (p. 29)

ACKNOWLEDGMENTS

First of all, thank you to the entire staff and community at Nomadic Press for publishing my first poetry collection. Big shout out to Maw Shien Win, my editor, for being so gracious, supportive, and encouraging during the process. To my daughter, Odessa, I am so fortunate to have you dancing beautifully and ferociously at my side the whole entire way — THANK YOU for your love, your bright spirit, your vibrance, your incredibly unique sparkle, and for joining me in this artistic life! Biggest heartfelt gratitude to my grandmother Marion. Thank you for putting the pen in my left hand, for giving me journals at Christmas every year, for telling me how much of a "hot ticket" I am, and for the best, most audible phone hugs at the end of every call. Cheers to my brother, Carter, for always making me laugh and keeping me sane in the weirdest of ways. Chuck, thanks for being a dedicated uncle through all the twists and turns, and for never giving up on me. Catherine Grace Rockwood and Charles Francis Ganem — for being such interesting people, snowed in together during the Great Storm of '78 — nine months before I was born. Hooray for the creative storms! Outpouring of love and appreciation to my friends, blood relatives, and chosen family — Bay Area, Hawaii, Alaska, New England, New York, Lebanon, and elsewhere — who have supported me in various ways, big and small, on my path as a creative, and in the becoming of this book. *To name a few of you*: Amanda M, Amy B, Anda S, Andre G, Anna S, Annika H, Aquiela MLR, Audrey W, Brenda

G, Brendon (from the Beat Museum), Dawn P, Dena R, Dylan K, Elaine B, Estelle C, Gabriel L, Heidi LP, Jerry C, J. K., Julie TU, Kay M, Khaia R, Kimberly K, Kimi S, KRM, Marine K, Mia R, Mike B, MKC, Nicole H, Paul CR, Rachel E, Rachel K, Regina L, RJ Equality, Robyn B, Rosa DA, Sara W, Soraiya, Steve D, Sylvia S, Tongo EM, the Vigils, and so many more... Chandler, Ogden, Cyndi and Chrissy and Gigi (all in absentia RIP). To all the creatives, the lovers, and those fighting against all odds — HATS OFF — And finally, thank you to the following literary reviews, journals, and magazines that gave these poems first homes on their way to being published with Nomadic Press in *Hot Thicket*!

The Lifted Brow, Peculiar: a queer literary journal, Reed Magazine, Red Savina Literary Review, Oakland Review, Riprap Journal, Eunoia Review, The Write Launch, The Normal School, New Delta Review, The Poet's Billow, Common Ground Review, and San Francisco Library: poem of the day

Cassandra Rockwood Ghanem

Cassandra Rockwood Ghanem is an award-winning writer and illustrator, whose poetry, creative nonfiction, and visual art have been published internationally. Her work has been featured in *Reed Magazine, The Normal School, New Delta Review, Rip Rap, The Lifted Brow, Beyond Words,* and elsewhere. She was recently selected for fellowships and awards from the Center for Book Arts in New York City and Disquiet International Literary Program in Portugal. In 2019, Cassandra founded a reading series at the Beat Museum in San Francisco, and in 2020 she illustrated *Basho's Haiku Journeys*, a picture book chronicling the life of Edo Period poet Matsuo Basho. She received her BA from California Institute of Integral Studies and MFA from California College of the Arts.

OTHER WAYS TO SUPPORT NOMADIC PRESS' WRITERS

In 2020, two funds geared specifically toward supporting our writers were created: the **Nomadic Press Black Writers Fund** and the **Nomadic Press Emergency Fund.**

The former is a forever fund that puts money directly into the pockets of our Black writers. The latter provides dignity-centered emergency grants to any of our writers in need.

Please consider supporting these funds. You can also more generally support Nomadic Press by donating to our general fund via nomadicpress.org/donate and by continuing to buy our books. As always, thank you for your support!

Scan below for more information and/or to donate.
You can also donate at nomadicpress.org/store.